P9-DTC-250

In Praise of
AUSTRALIAN
NATIONAL
PARKS

# In Praise of AUSTRALIAN NATIONAL PARKS

Introduced by Vincent Serventy

# Contents



*Endpapers: The Glasshouse Mountains at sunset, southern Queensland*

*Page 1: Wittenoom Gorge, Hamersley Range National Park, Western Australia*

*Pages 2 & 3: Stirling Range landscape, Stirling Range National Park, Western Australia*

*Left: Mt Warning and the Tweed River, Mt Warning State Park, New South Wales*

*Right: The Horn, Mt Buffalo National Park, Victoria*

# 'For all the people forever'

'In wildness is the preservation of the world.'

In these words Henry Thoreau, a famous American writer of the last century, expressed the philosophy which is at the heart of the national park movement. He summed up his experiences in the forests and marshes of his native land with the following passage:

'We need the tonic of wildness, to wade sometimes in marshes where the bittern and the meadow-hen lurk, and hear the booming of the snipe. . . At the same time that we are earnest to explore all things, we require that all things be mysterious and unexplorable, that land and sea be infinitely wild, unsurveyed, unfathomed by us because unfathomable. We can never have enough of nature.'

Early man was a hunter-gatherer, surrounded by a landscape of the kind enjoyed by the Australian Aborigines. With the rise of agricultural man the world of nature was slowly pushed back. Forests melted before the farmer's firestick and axe, and bushland before his plough.

In this sea of agriculture some felt the need for the kind of wildness where they could recreate themselves free of the pressures of a man-made world. For the rich and powerful the solution came in the deliberate making of preserves, a famous one being the New Forest in England produced for the pleasure of William the Conqueror. Although used for hunting it also had the advantage of offering a feeling of wildness. The poet William Wordsworth speaking of his beloved Lake District in northern England advanced the then novel idea that here was a national property in which 'every man has a right and interest'.

*Crystal Creek, near Paluma, Crystal Creek National Park, Queensland*

The American philosopher Ralph Waldo Emerson met Wordsworth and they may have discussed nature as part of public property. Emerson was also the friend and patron of Thoreau and so a chain of ideas linked the past with the present and the old world with the new.

Influenced by such ideas the modern concept of a national park crystallised around a campfire in the State of Wyoming in 1870. Among a party of visitors enthralled by the natural wonders they had seen in this wilderness was Cornelius Hedges.

An American who had been influenced by the writings of Thoreau he exclaimed that here was an area of land that should be 'set aside as a park for all the people forever'. Two years later the United States Congress turned this dream into a reality when the world's first national park was created.

Seven years later on the other side of the world in New South Wales the government set aside an area of bushland which became the nucleus of the present Royal National Park. Most present day Australian 'national' parks in the strict sense are State parks, since only the Federal. Government can act for the nation. Yet if the parks keep the ideal of the original Yellowstone National Park in Wyoming, the word is valid.

In this century the national park idea burgeoned and a recent United Nations Report listed 892 national parks in 94 countries.

The International Union for the Conservation of Nature drew up guidelines which stated that a national park must have adequate governmental protection, be effectively managed and of such a size that its integrity may be preserved.

In Australia the fourth annual conference of State ministers responsible for national parks accepted that: 'A National Park is a relatively large area, set aside for its features of predominantly unspoiled natural landscape, flora and fauna, permanently dedicated for public enjoyment, education and inspiration and protected from all interference other than essential management practices, so that its natural attributes are preserved.' and this embodies what most people feel is a national park.

Today every State has a National Park Service and there is also an Australian Service for areas under federal control. The number of our national parks runs into many hundreds and each year more are added.

Although about two per cent of the Australian land area has now been dedicated this is still only one-half of the internationally accepted minimum of five per cent which should be reserved — not any five per cent but an area which includes carefully selected samples of all the variety a country possesses in terms of landscape and wildlife. Equally significant is that such an area ensures that no person will be more than a day's drive from at least one national park. Where parks occupy an area less than this and are concentrated in a remote location, many people are deprived of the chance to enjoy the values a national park has to offer.

The desire for enjoyment creates problems. A very apt phrase is 'loving a park to death'. Too many people may destroy what they came to enjoy. Although there are only minor problems in Australia, some national parks abroad face difficulties. In Japan one park has seventy-two million visitors a year, a staggering load for any natural area to carry without degradation.

In most cases zoning can keep a large section free of heavy use and this is the plan adopted in Australia. Many areas are closed to cars while, increasingly, accommodation is being offered on the edge of parks rather than inside them.

There is an increasing demand for the creation of 'English' or landscape parks where agriculture, industry and the homes of man are all part of the reserve. What is kept inviolate is the look of the countryside and changes are examined in terms of keeping the integrity of the whole.

National parks are not the beginning and end of nature conservation and recreation in natural areas. The headlong growth of recreation needs has caused governments to look at novel methods of satisfying demands which range from people who want to stroll through bushland and picnic, and energetic climbers who want to scale mountains to horse-riders, trail-bike riders and water skiers.

There is no one solution. Wilderness areas, nature reserves, State forests and pine plantations (which have a particular appeal to recent European arrivals) all cater for many different activities. A new concept of recreation parks is being tried in New South Wales, using landscapes lacking national park quality but ideal for taking pressure from more sensitive areas.

Although basically concerned with people and their recreation national parks are often essential to the preservation of plant and animal species which today can survive only in well managed areas of bushland. Such 'banks' of unique species are important as stores of genetic material which may be needed to improve our crop plants and animals.

There is no doubt that these accelerating and diverse demands will call for the greatest professional skills in management. We must plan, not just for a few years ahead, but for the Australia of the next century. We hold this land in trust to be handed to future generations, we hope with the beauty of the present day and with some mistakes of the past repaired. Our national parks are an essential feature of an environment of a high quality.

*Right: The Pinnacles, Nambung National Park, Western Australia*

*Below: Katherine Gorge National Park, Northern Territory*

# Treasury of ancient landscapes

## NORTHERN WESTERN AUSTRALIA & NORTHERN TERRITORY

This vast area covering one third of the continent falls into two distinct parts. The southern half stretching from the west coast to the central deserts is dominated by the great plateau, a shield of ancient rocks some being among the oldest on earth. In the central deserts these rocks are often covered with sand which creates a red desert landscape.

Thousands of years ago the inland was even drier than it is today and the ever-shifting sands were shaped into dunes by a vast anticyclonic swirl of wind which dominated the central Australian climate.

High sand ridges developed along the path of the wind and some run for hundreds of kilometres in one direction without a break. With the slight increase in rainfall in more recent years the plants took hold and grew freely enough to stop the sand moving, fixing the dunes found there today. Only the vivid red crests show where the plants have not yet won the battle and some sand still blows before the wind.

Jutting like islands out of this sea of sand are rocks and mountains, the most famous being Ayers Rock and the Olgas. These are not giant pebbles lying on the surface but island mountains, the tips of masses of rock buried beneath the surface.

This southern section, with its low rainfall, has long been the least populated part of Australia. Even the Aborigines who first colonised this arid country were thinly spaced and travelled vast distances to hunt animals and gather occasional harvests of seeds and fruits; on this almost continuous walkabout depended their survival.

The ancient landscape remained almost unchanged by man until in the last few years the discovery of mineral treasures caused an upheaval in the western section. New towns sprang up and in places the works of man are starting to rival the works of nature in their immensity.

In central Australia a new flood of humanity has changed the pattern of life, but these are seekers after another treasure; tourists looking for excitement, and refreshment of spirit, in the red desert.

The northern half of this area is mainly a huge plateau of uplifted land whose rocks, although old, are not as ancient as those of the southern shield. They too hold mineral treasures, the most recently sought being uranium ores. Rivers have carved this high land, making it one of the most rugged areas in Australia.

The Kimberley coast is swept by vast tidal movements. The rise and fall of the water, reaching thirteen metres, creates currents which make this a most dangerous coastline.

Heavy monsoonal rains in summer, with a winter dry season, develop a rich and varied plant and animal life able to support a large Aboriginal population.

The combination of a dangerous coast, a rugged inland and vigorous and aggressive Aborigines kept the northwest relatively unchanged until the beginning of this century.

Large reserves such as those in Arnhem Land and in the Kimberleys have allowed some Aborigines to continue their old way of life. Their skill in dance, song and painting has helped lead to a new understanding of the richness of a culture which was ruthlessly destroyed over most of the continent.

Supreme among their achievements were the paintings in the rock art galleries, acclaimed by anthropologists and artists as being among the world's finest. Today the galleries are regarded as among the treasures of Australia's heritage.

The coastal plains are the homes of myriads of waterbirds. Magpie geese, brolgas and ducks with kangaroos, wallabies and other wildlife are making tourism one of the major industries of the north.

*Right: Cape Range National Park, Western Australia*

*Over page: Murchison River, Kalbarri National Park, Western Australia*

# Western gorges

Situated approximately sixteen kilometres from Fitzroy Crossing, Geikie Gorge (above) is set in a three kilometres-wide strip of land bisected by Western Australia's mighty Fitzroy River.

Among the iron mountains that stretch through the Pilbarra district lies the Hamersley Range National Park. Covering 590 206 hectares, the park is large by national standards and contains four main gorges: Hamersley, Dale, Yampire and Wittenoom seen here (right) in an unusual aerial photograph.

# Dividing line

The Tropic of Capricorn cuts the continent in half, following a line from Rockhampton in the east to just north of Salt Lake on Western Australia's Indian Ocean coast. To the centre, and south-east of this cartographic line, is the Simpson Desert (above and left) which covers 145 000 square kilometres. The desert extends through the Northern Territory, Queensland and South Australia and national parks have been established in the two States. Surprisingly, the desert supports a multitude of animals and birds, and the infrequent rains are followed by a profusion of wildflowers.

Three kilometres north of Alice Springs, a small historic site preserves the relics of the first settlement in the area (above right). Constructed over a century ago, a repeater station was built as an integral link in the overland telegraph line to Darwin. Further north, near Wauchope, the Stuart Highway bisects a scenic reserve featuring the Devil's Marbles (right) — a collection of high, granite boulders, sculpted by the elements over the years.

# The gargantuans

The landmarks and formations of the 'Centre' are perhaps better recognised by overseas visitors — and indeed Australians — than the artefacts of modern Australia. Synonymous with the area is, of course, Ayers Rock and, to a lesser extent, the Olgas.

Both these rock gargantuans form the Uluru National Park which covers an area of 126 132 hectares and is located about 450 kilometres south-west of Alice Springs. The park is accessible by gravelled road to the adventurous traveller or by the more leisurely means of coach or air tours operating from Alice Springs.

Ayers Rock rises to a height of 348 metres and is some nine kilometres in circumference. The Rock is worth more than a cursory glance: an overnight stay may well let the visitor experience the Rock's varying moods (over page left) — colours can change from sunrise to sunset through a spectrum of pinks, reds, oranges, crimsons and purples.

Thirty-two kilometres west of Ayers Rock a series of domes rises from the arid plain to form the Olgas (left). Like the Rock, the boulder-like mountains change vividly in colour depending on the varying light of the day.

Both the formations were deposited around 600 million years ago during the Cambrian period. Closer to our own time scale Uluru (Ayers Rock) and Katatjuta (the Olgas) have featured significantly in the ritual life and myths of the Aboriginal Yankuntjatjara and Pitjandjara tribes.

To the east and west of Alice Springs can be found the Macdonnell Ranges (over page right). These hard, quartzite ridges straggle the landscape for over 300 kilometres. Initially they are deceptive: further investigation reveals that the Ranges cradle small, yet fascinating, parks and scenic reserves.

# Gaps & gorges

Dotted throughout the Northern Territory's Macdonnell Ranges can be found some of the most spectacular terrain in the nation's centre. At the north-west of the range a tributary of the Finke River feeds the pools in the gorge at Ormiston National Park (right). Nearby, the Glen Helen (over page, above right) and Serpentine gorges (over page, left) complement Ormiston. Although they are smaller, the river system has again carved its way through the Macdonnells and pools reflect the magnificent strata of red rock. Close to, and south-east of Alice Springs, the road to the Ross River passes Jessie (below) and Emily Gaps: two short rugged gorges with sparse vegetation. A few kilometres to the north, the Valley of Eagles joins Trephina Gorge (over page, below right) — a gorge enhanced after rain which forms pools to give the impression of an oasis.

# Safari country

To the east of Darwin, toward the South and East Alligator Rivers and Arnhem Land, lies Australia's 'safari country'. This is the land of crocodiles, buffaloes, kangaroos and of billabongs teeming with bird life. At one time it was the preserve of the professional hunter but today the area has been opened to the visitor seeking either a one-day tour or an extended wild-life tour during the 'dry' from May through to October.

East of the Katherine township, on the river of the same name, lies a spectacular gorge — the focal point of the Katherine Gorge National Park.

During the dry season a trip in a small boat will show the gorge in its true perspective. The sheer rock walls drop from 100 metres to be lapped by the waters of the Katherine River, while the combination of sunlight and shadow reflect a myriad of colours. However, the gorge has two faces and with the onset of the wet season, tranquillity gives way to the river's rushing torrents.

*Above: Nourlangie Rock on the border of Kakadu National Park west of Arnhem Land.*

*Right: Katherine Gorge National Park, 350 kilometres south-east of Darwin.*

# Unspoiled scenery preserved

## NEW SOUTH WALES, EASTERN VICTORIA & TASMANIA

The southeast corner holds the majority of the Australian people in an urban sprawl stretching almost unbroken from Melbourne to Newcastle, the first European settlements being made on this fertile shore.

The dramatic coastline is regarded as being among the most beautiful in the world and man added to the scene by building small towns along the beaches with their towering headlands and backdrop of massive ranges. Tasmania is an excellent example of a mountainous island enhanced by many fine small towns with attractive old buildings.

There is still much unspoiled scenery preserved in the national parks. Southwest Tasmania has a variety of forest including temperate rainforest with large stands of Antarctic beech, as well as buttongrass plains whose monotony is broken by many peaks and lakes.

Sir Edmund Hillary described this area as the best walking country in the world and the same is true of much of southeastern Australia. Plans are in hand to create a giant tri-State walking trail starting in the Victorian Highlands and snaking northward along the Great Dividing Range to Cape York.

Two million years ago the last great period of mountain building took place in Australia and left Mt Kosciusko in New South Wales as our highest point at 2230 metres high, although Mt Buller and Mt Hotham in Victoria are only slightly lower. These high country areas contain the bulk of our snowfields, today thronged in winter with ski-ing enthusiasts. Increasingly they are also becoming summer tourist havens since the soils here produce a wealth of late summer wildflowers.

Although Australia is now a quiet place in terms of earthquakes and volcanoes it was not always so. The great western plain of Victoria is formed from lavas and volcanic ash and is regarded as the third largest of its kind in the world.

Some of these lavas are five million years old, but others are recent. Tower Hill was once an active volcano and ceased activity only some 5000 years ago, a recency it shared with Mt Gambier in South Australia. The Aborigines of the area witnessed some exciting eruptions and added them to their legends.

Along the southern edge of this volcanic plain is spectacular coastal scenery. Over thousands of years the soft, horizontal sediments have worn away under steady attack by the sea to produce a series of landforms with natural bridges, arches and stacks the most prominent. Those near Port Campbell are the best known and are included in a national park.

In New South Wales volcanoes of fifteen million years ago created the spectacular landforms of the Warrumbungles and the ranges of the Kaputar National Park.

Inland from the coastal high country is a vast inland plain covered by wandering river systems, huge in size if not in the quantity of the waters they carry. Since half of Australia is less than 300 metres above sea level, and only a twentieth more than 600 metres, this flatness leads to slowmoving rivers which in times of flood may spread many kilometres away from their normal channels.

The Murray and Darling Rivers with their tributaries drain an area of about one million square kilometres, possibly the largest drainage basin in the world. Because of the vast area, and the occasional flooding creating huge swamps, it is the most important nursery of waterbirds in Australia.

The forests which grow along the rivers are the home of grey kangaroos while the red kangaroos find a haven in the open country. In good seasons myriads of birds turn the seas of grass into a vast aviary.

Although in many parts of Australia the sight or sound of people causes most wildlife to take cover, often to emerge only in the shelter of darkness, national parks such as Kinchega have led to a new confidence. Here the visual extinction which so much of our wildlife suffers has gone and the park is like a Garden of Eden.

*Right: The Needles, Gibraltar Range National Park, north-eastern New South Wales.*

*Over page: Distinctive ridges of the Warrumbungle National Park, New South Wales.*

# Sydney surrounds

Because of their close proximity to Sydney the Ku-ring-gai Chase and Brisbane Water National parks are becoming more and more popular. Both parks are situated in the picturesque Hawkesbury River area. Ku-ring-gai Chase (left) is renowned for its creeks, inlets and bushland walking tracks. Further north, near Gosford, Brisbane Water features 100-metre sandstone cliffs rising above the flooded valleys of the Hawkesbury (above).

Still on the New South Wales coast, but approximately 225 kilometres north of Brisbane Water, can be found the lake system and dunes of Myall Lakes (below right).

Seventy kilometres west of Sydney the Blue Mountains give their name to a 100 770 hectares national park characterised by glens, waterfalls and blue gum forest. The Three Sisters (above right) are the best known landmark within the range. These remarkable towers of weathered sandstone rise above the slopes of the Jamieson Valley at Katoomba.

# Alpine resorts

The mere mention of Mt Kosciusko immediately creates images of Australia's winter playground. And with some justification, as Kosciusko National Park can boast the most extensive snowfields in the nation. During the short winter, snowfalls of two metres and drifts up to nine metres have been known in blizzards which occasionally sweep the Australian Alps. The most popular and developed ski resorts are at Thredbo (above), Smiggin Holes and Perisher Valley.

However, skiing is not the only attraction; alpine tracks and rugged terrain (such as the Ramshead Range, right), fishing, riding, the flora and, of course, the pervading alpine splendour further enhance the area's popularity.

Kosciusko is the largest national park in New South Wales and contains Mts Kosciusko, Townsend (left), Twynam and Carruthers; the only peaks in Australia to rise above the 7 000 feet (2 114 metre) mark. Stretching from the Capital Territory in the north-east southwards to the Victorian border, the park covers an area of 611 500 hectares.

# Scenic backdrop

Mt Buffalo National Park is eastern Victoria's answer to Kosciusko. Snug in the Australian Alps this granite plateau is a favourite winter resort for skiing enthusiasts. In warmer weather, its scenic backdrop of peaks, valleys and streams provides an excellent venue for walks and riding.

By contrast, the ferns and other rainforest flora of the Tarra Valley National Park (right) in the Strzelecki Ranges of East Gippsland is only some 127 hectares. Lyrebirds are numerous and the park sets out to preserve the fauna and flora native to the area.

Eildon Reservoir's man-made shore line has been made available for public use and is the basis of Fraser National Park (below). One hundred and forty-five kilometres north-east of Melbourne, Eildon provides excellent facilities for holidays, aquatic sports and angling.

*Left: Mt Buffalo National Park's Lake Catani (above) and granite domes (below).*

# Lakes & inlets

The eastern half of Victoria's coastline boasts numerous parks, the best known being Wilson's Promontory (right) — a mountainous peninsula with a diversity of granite headlands, white beaches and forests. The park, 240 kilometres south-east of Melbourne, attracts thousands of people each year with its opportunities for fishing, surfing and camping.

To the far east of Victoria's coastline, near the New South Wales border, Mallacoota Inlet National Park (left) preserves the beautiful hills, islands and forests that surround the deeply indented shoreline.

*Above: The Lakes National Park set among the lakes behind the surf beaches of Gippsland's Ninety-Mile Beach.*

*Right: Squeaky Beach (above) and Oberon Bay (below), Wilson's Promontory.*

# Rugged beauty

In proportion to its area, Tasmania has been well endowed with parks, reserves and historic sites. The State has both the scenery and the history for the creation of such areas, evidence of which can be seen on the Tasman Peninsula to the south-east. Here the Convict Coal Mines and famous Port Arthur historic sites are visited by thousands of tourists each year. For sheer rugged beauty Tasman Island (right) and Eaglehawk Neck are well worth a visit.

*Below: The 1 430 metres peak of Frenchman's Cap which gives its name to the national park near the Lyell Highway to the west of Tasmania.*

# Tarns & tors

Until the enlargement of the Lake Pedder area, Cradle Mountain-Lake St Clair was the largest national park within Tasmania. The park is impressive and covers an area of 126 000 hectares which contain much of the State's most spectacular scenery of gorges, waterfalls, tarns and numerous lakes. Mt Ossa, which at 1 617 metres is the highest mountain in the State, is among more than twenty-five peaks in the region. The park can be traversed by a walking track from the Cradle Valley in the north to Lake St Clair in the south. Along the track unattended huts have been placed for the convenience of those bushwalkers willing to accept the challenge of the eighty-five kilometre route.

By the end of 1976 over 403 000 hectares had been gazetted for the South West National Park (right), providing the largest area of wilderness in Tasmania. It also has some of the best bushwalking country in the nation, and although there are a number of well mapped paths to certain areas, the terrain should be approached with caution.

*Left: Dove Lake and Cradle Mountain (above) and Crater Lake (below) of Cradle Mountain-Lake St Clair National Park.*

*Right: The Wilmot Range from Lake Pedder (above) and Federation Peak (below), the goal of many climbers from all over the country.*

# Steep headlands

Together with Mt Field, Freycinet Peninsula (right), on Tasmania's central eastern coast, was created as a national park in 1916. Just over fifty years later in 1967 Schouten Island was added to give the park an area of nearly 11 000 hectares.

The peninsula's coastline has both steep headlands and sandy beaches while the centre of this promontory rises in granite peaks — the highest being Mt Freycinet at 614 metres. Light vegetation can be seen in profusion and it is probable that a hundred species of orchids can be found. Animals native to Tasmania are plentiful and the native cat and tiger cat are in evidence.

The uninhabited Schouten Island lies off the southern tip of the peninsula and access is by charter boat. A fault line from north to south bisects the island into dolerite on the west and granite on the east, and marks an abrupt vegetation change of, respectively, parkland and thorny scrub. During the last century a whaling station was established and modest tin and coal mining ventures were attempted.

# Historic island

In 1825 Maria Island (above) was set aside for a penal settlement but was abandoned for this purpose in 1832. Eleven years later the island was re-opened and served as a probation station until 1850. It was in this later period that brick buildings were created by convict labour: the relics of those of historical significance have now been restored. From 1850 the island has been used for grazing and, for a short period, the manufacturing of cement.

Many native Tasmanian animals, including the forester kangaroo, were introduced in the late 'sixties and in 1971 this 9 672 hectare island off Tasmania's eastern coast was declared a national park.

*Left: Port Arthur, Tasman Peninsula*

*Right: The cascading waters of Russell Falls in the Mount Field National Park, central southern Tasmania*

# State of tropical contrasts

## MAINLY QUEENSLAND

In the northeast of Australia rises the cream of Australian wildlife. No other State can compare with Queensland in the rich variety of its natural history. On its western borders it has a national park in the red dunes of the Simpson Desert. From here one travels eastward through the extraordinary Channel Country where braided streams take water south to Lake Eyre.

In the vast swamps and desert sands which soak up this water heavy rains bring outpourings of wild life. Some species such as the longhaired rat develop in plague proportions in the rare good seasons.

Still further eastward are vast areas of grassland, mulga and brigalow. In central Queensland is the Carnarvon Ranges National Park. This beautiful area is noted for its Aboriginal paintings and is also interesting because the sandstone blocks are part of the aquifers of the Great Artesian Basin.

Further eastward in the mountainous areas of the Great Dividing Range grow magnificent forests, and in the more sheltered and wetter sections, rainforest.

This closed forest is also known as jungle, brush and scrub. The Australian section is part of a huge, green belt which encircles the continents of the earth in the warmer, wetter areas of the globe. This habitat was the home of man when he evolved probably during the last two million years. The crowns of the trees form a green canopy which shuts out the blue sky and dims the world below. Here is a vast reservoir of plants where each hectare contains hundreds of species compared to the dozens found in drier forests.

The green world is created by a combination of factors such as soil and temperature but above all high rainfall. While the tall trees dominate the canopy, woody lianes drape across the branches below reaching towards the light. There are also deciduous trees, unusual plants in Australia, with many palms in the wetter soils.

From north to south, and also depending on height above sea level, there are variations in the rainforest. Along the northern coastlines are monsoonal forests evolved to survive a winter dry season; in the Cooktown to Ingham area true tropical rainforest, with some patches further south; from here subtropical forest extends to northern New South Wales. Finally the cool temperate rainforests of the Lamington National Park extend south into the forests of East Gippsland in Victoria and Tasmania.

As well as the variety of plants there is an equally bewildering variety of animals — ranging from giant birds such as the cassowary, to the tree-climbing kangaroo blundering through the treetops.

Offshore, stretching 2000 kilometres from Gladstone and north to New Guinea is the Great Barrier Reef, some 200 000 square kilometres in area.

This extraordinary structure has developed during the last 15 000 years and in the vast home produced by the growth of minute reef-building coral polyps, other life thrives. It is the combination of coral beauty and the multitudes of other marine creatures which makes these reefs one of the wonders of the world.

Below water is a rich world, and above it are many fascinating islands. Some are sections of the mainland cut off by a rising sealevel while others are true coral cays born of the sea from fragments of coral skeletons and those of other marine creatures.

The two best known of these cays are Heron Island and Green Island, both national parks catering for some of the hundreds of thousands of people who throng to this coral wonderland. Perhaps the Great Barrier Reef can be regarded as the main gem in the crown of jewels which make up our national park system.

*Right: The beaches and mangroves of Hinchinbrook Island off the northern Queensland coast*

*Over page: Shute Harbour, Conway National Park, view to Long Island, central Queensland coast.*

# Coral wonders

Covering an area of 200 000 square kilometres, the Great Barrier Reef is the world's largest group of coral reefs. This collection of atolls, cays, islands and underwater reefs extends from Torres Strait south along the Queensland coast to just below the Tropic of Capricorn. Many of the islands are flourishing as holiday resorts but, not surprisingly, many have had large tracts designated as national parks.

*Left above: Exposed coral*

*Left below: Pentecost Island from Lindeman Island National Park, central Queensland coast*

*Right above: Bauer Bay, South Molle Island, in the Whitsunday Passage, central Queensland coast*

*Right below: Coastal view from Lindeman Island*

# Majestic peak

*Above: The spectacular waterfall at Wallaman Falls National Park, north-eastern Queensland, where the water plummets for 300 metres to be dispersed by the rocks in the rainforest below.*

*Right: The Pinnacle is the name given to the towering peak that majestically rises above the palms in the Cape Hillsborough National Park. Forty-five kilometres north of Mackay and overlooking the Hills-borough Channel off Queensland's central coast, the park is a montage of rugged seashores, caves and hills. There are facilities for camping, together with picnic areas and ample opportunities for bush-walking, fishing and swimming.*

# A grand gallery

'The Grand Canyon of Queensland' has been one of the descriptions given to Carnarvon Gorge (right), the main feature of this national park being the gorge from which it takes its name. The park covers 26 900 hectares and lies on the eastern slopes of the Great Dividing Range about 400 kilometres inland from Bundaberg. The gorge, through which the Carnarvon Creek flows, is some thirty-two kilometres long and varies from 46 to 365 metres in width, with sandstone cliffs up to 183 metres high. Of particular interest are the caves — containing excellent examples of Aboriginal paintings — that are dotted throughout the Carnarvons.

*Above: Robinson Gorge National Park, the inland park that spans Robinson Creek, a headwater tributary of the Dawson River.*

# River circuits

Eungella National Park, eighty kilometres west of Mackay on Queensland's central coast, is typified by its tall palms and abundant undergrowth. Many kilometres of circuit tracks take the visitor by the Broken River (above) through sections of forests and by pools to lookouts over the Pioneer Valley.

*Left: The crater lake of Lake Barrine National Park of the Atherton Tableland on Queensland's northern coast*

*Above right: Black Mountain National Park, near Cooktown, Cape York Peninsula*

*Below right: Palmerston National Park, which contains 2 586 hectares of tropical rainforest, overlooks the Johnstone River and is thirty-two kilometres from Innisfail.*

# Striking spires

South from Bundaberg down to the New South Wales border more than forty parks enhance Queensland's south-east corner.

Seventy kilometres north of Brisbane some of the most striking formations of pillars and peaks in the region can be seen — the Glasshouse Mountains. The range consists of eight main peaks with numerous outcrops and foothills. Perhaps the most familiar of these are Mts Coonowrin and Beerwah (right). These two peaks, together with Ngungun and Tibrogargan, have been set aside as national parks to ensure their preservation. The parks, accessible from the Bruce Highway, are undeveloped and are suitable for rock-climbing and naturalist groups.

*Over page, above left: Mt Lindesay, which gives its name to a small national park on the Queensland and New South Wales border*

*Below left: Springbrook National Park, comprising the small parks of Warrie, Gwongorella, Mt Cougal and a park numbered 1 083, south-east Queensland*

*Right: Cascading over 100 metres into a valley rainforest, the waterfall in Kondalilla National Park is the main feature of this 75-hectare park near Nambour in south-east Queensland.*

# Nut festival

Cunningham's Gap (left) is of historic significance. It was named after Alan Cunningham who travelled over the pass during his search in 1828 for a passage from the coast to the Darling Downs — the fertile plains of which he discovered the previous year. This area of eucalypt and rainforest on the Great Dividing Range now forms a national park of some 3 000 hectares and is situated on the Cunningham Highway, 110 kilometres west of Brisbane.

Also of historic significance in Aboriginal culture are the Bunya Mountains. It was in the vicinity of Mt Mowbullan that the tribes of south-east Queensland would congregate to feast on the milky-white nuts of the bunya pine. The festivals lasted for weeks during which time tribal demarcations and hostilities were suspended. Today this section of the Great Dividing Range forms the 11 610-hectare Bunya Mountains National Park.

*Below left: A panoramic view from Lamington National Park toward Mt Lindesay*

*Above right: Grass trees of the Bunya Mountains*

*Below right: Mt Barney National Park, which complements its sister parks of Mts Lindesay and Maroon, on the Queensland border with New South Wales*

# Landscapes of fantastic beauty

## SOUTH AUSTRALIA, WESTERN VICTORIA & SOUTHERN WESTERN AUSTRALIA

The southern half of Western Australia is part of the great shield of ancient rocks, an area of great mineral wealth, once treasured for gold and today for nickel. This plateau drops sharply to a coastal plain which stretches from near the Murchison River around the coast to the South Australian border.

The great plateau is covered in the east by the sand ridges of the Great Victoria Desert. South of this is the vast limestone plateau of the Nullarbor Plain, one of the most striking landforms in Australia. It is overwhelming by its sheer monotony of thousands of kilometres where nothing taller than a shrub breaks the surface.

The plains finally give way in South Australia to the line of hills of the Flinders Ranges, part of a rocky backbone which reaches as far south as Mount Lofty, the backdrop of Adelaide. To the north of the Flinders is the 'horseshoe' of lakes of which Lake Eyre is the largest and most famous.

The coastline from west to east is a deceptively gentle rim of sandy beaches and dunes with a few limestone cliffs. The most dramatic of these front the Great Australian Bight, the abrupt edge of the limestone of the Nullarbor Plain.

The offshore shallow waters with many reefs provided an unfriendly welcome to the first European navigators. Some of these Dutch explorers ventured far to the east in search of fertile country with possibilities for trade but the dryness and lack of harbours discouraged them and this southwestern section of Australia was left almost untouched until the last century. Today the same reefs are providing new wealth in the form of spiny crayfish which find the limestone of the underwater rocks an ideal living area.

With its profusion of wildflowers Western Australia deserves the title of the Wildflower State. The long isolation of the southwest corner allowed the plants to evolve great diversity. Today about three thousand species are concentrated here and among them a quarter are found nowhere else in the world. Only South Africa can match this wildflower wonderland.

In the wetter southwest corner there are forests of a tall eucalypt, the karri, which rivals the beauty of the ash forests of the southeast. Here also is limestone country with many caves whose development of cave 'ornaments' makes them among the most beautiful in the world.

While the western section has its wealth of wildflowers South Australia offers other attractions. With its ancient rocks and in places, ancient landscapes, it is a geologist's paradise. The vast system of salt lakes contains thousands of fossils, skeletons of marsupials preserved in the mud. Among these are the remains of a giant diprotodon, an animal the size of a hippopotamus, a three metre tall kangaroo and a marsupial lion equal in size to the lion species which today wanders the plains of Africa.

The high country of the Flinders Ranges attracts by the beauty of its landforms and the river red gums which line the creeks have been made famous by the paintings of Hans Heysen. Wilpena Pound National Park in the height of the holiday season has a camping area the size of a small country town.

In the southeast corner Mount Gambier and its blue lake offers a reminder that this was once a place of fiery volcanoes which poured out lava and ash.

To the north the desert areas blossom after heavy rains and Lake Eyre, for over a hundred years a wilderness of salt and sand, has filled twice in the last thirty years, creating a landscape of fantastic beauty. More and more visitors travel northward in the winter to enjoy the striking wildlife of this country and the fascination of the desert landscape.

*The 1 135-metre peak of Point Bonney, Wilpena Pound, in South Australia's Flinders Ranges National Park.*

*Over page: Wilpena from Bunyeroo, Flinders Ranges.*

# Mountain vistas

South Australia provides perhaps some of the finest mountain scenery in the nation. The Flinders Ranges emerge in the State's mid-north and run into the central deserts of the continent. Among the ranges are the Gammon, Mt Remarkable, Telowie Gorge and Flinders Ranges National Parks. The latter contains the spectacular Wilpena Pound, an immense basin ringed by sheer cliffs and jagged ridges. Also within the park to the north of the Pound, and well worth a visit, are the Bunyeroo and Brachina gorges. For the experienced bushwalker, the rough and remote Gammon Ranges to the north of the Flinders present a challenge.

Within reach of Adelaide are the Morialta Falls Reserve (far left) and Cleland Conservation Park and Belair Recreation Park set in the Mt Lofty Ranges, overlooking the city.

One hundred and twelve kilometres south of Adelaide lies Kangaroo Island. Situated at the island's western extremity is the Flinders Chase National Point. At Kirkpatrick Point are the Remarkable Rocks (over page left). These granite boulders, strangely sculptured by the elements, balance precariously on a smooth granite dome which on one side abruptly plunges into the Southern Ocean.

Directly north at Innes National Park, on the mainland's Yorke Peninsula, lies the wreck of the 771-ton Norwegian iron barque, 'Ethel' (over page, below right). Driven ashore in 1904, she was one of the many vessels to founder on South Australia's Yorke Peninsula coast.

The word 'Coorong' is a corruption of the Aboriginal 'Karangh', meaning 'narrow neck', and the description would adequately fit the 100-kilometre long, two kilometre-wide lake on the Younghusband Peninsula. Nearly 13 000 hectares now make up the Coorong National Park and Game Reserve (over page, above right) — renowned for its sand dunes and shallow carbonate lakes. About 160 species of birds have been recorded in the area.

*Above: Koalas in the Cleland Conservation Park.*

*Left: Sea-lion suckling pup. Colonies of Australian sea-lions, or hair seals, can be seen in the Seal Bay Conservation Park or Flinders Chase National Park, Kangaroo Island.*

# Configurations

The stormy seas of the Southern Ocean have lashed the coastal plains of western Victoria to form the vertical cliffs included in the narrow strip that comprises Port Campbell National Park. However, 'The Sentinels', the dramatic off-shore landforms (left), appear to stand defiantly against the relentless sea, while other aggregates of clay, sand and limestone have been sculptured into fascinating configurations such as 'The Archway' (right).

In contrast, further to the west, can be found the more tranquil waters of the Glenelg River (below) in the Glenelg National Park on Victoria's South Australian border.

# Mallee parks

In a line, and parallel to the South Australian border, are what could be described as Victoria's 'mallee parks': Hattah Lakes, Wyperfeld and the Little Desert. The biggest of them, and Victoria's largest park, is Wyperfeld (right) which covers around 56 600 hectares. The area preserves many species of flora and wildlife, the best-known of the latter being the mallee fowl. The Lowan, or mallee fowl, lays its eggs in mounds made of decaying vegetation and relies on the warmth generated by decomposition to incubate them.

Mallee scrub constitutes the largest part of Hattah Lakes (right, below) yet the lakes and billabongs support many indigenous animals and numerous water birds such as ducks, herons and spoonbills. Seen here (left and below) is the southernmost of the trio: the Little Desert National Park.

# Land of giants

As could be expected, the character of the parks in the south-west of Western Australia is in contrast to those of the north, as is the climate. Evidence of this is the plant life of the area, and in particular, the karri forests of such parks as Walpole-Nornalup, Warren (right) and Porongorup Range. These magnificent gums are one of the tallest trees in the southern hemisphere and can grow to eighty-five metres.

Captain James Stirling, Western Australia's first Governor, gave his name to a range that has in turn become the Stirling Range National Park (below). Within the 115 689 hectares of parkland rise several peaks, such as the 732-metre 'The Abbey' (left). These provide a fascinating splendour, especially during the spring when shrouded in mist yet carpeted with wildflowers.

About thirty-two kilometres east of Esperance the coastal Cape Le Grand National Park (over page) possesses a rugged coastline and ocean vistas of the Recherche Archipelago.

PHOTOGRAPHIC ACKNOWLEDGEMENTS

ROBIN SMITH: Front & back dust jacket; endpapers; 1; 2-3; 4; 6; 8; 9; 12-13; 17 (below); 23; 24; 27; 29; 30-31; 33 (above); 34; 35 (above); 37; 40-41; 42 (above); 43 (below); 47; 50-51; 52; 54; 55; 56-57; 60-61; 62 (above); 63; 64; 65; 67; 68-69; 70; 71; 72; 73 (below); 75; 78; JOCELYN BURT: 5; 18-19; 26; 33 (below); 38; 39; 42 (below); 43 (above); 44-45; 46 (above); 49; 53; 58 (above); 59; 73 (above); 74; 76 (above); 79; 80. JOHN CARNEMOLLA: 11; 32 (below); 46 (below); 58 (below); 62 (below). JOHN BROWNLIE: 14; 16; 17 (above); 21; 22; 32 (above); 35 (below); 36; 40; 56; 76 (below); 77. KEN STEPNELL: 20; 25. VISAIR EDUCATIONAL: 15.

Designed and produced by
John Currey, O'Neil Pty Ltd for
Rigby Limited
Adelaide Melbourne Sydney Brisbane Perth
First published in 1977
National Library of Australia Registry Card
Number and ISBN 0 7270 0530 8



Type set in Australia
Printed and bound in Singapore